Gold

Gold

Aenea Kanaan

RESOURCE *Publications* • Eugene, Oregon

GOLD

Resource Publications
An Imprint of Wipf and Stock Publishers
199 W. 8th Ave., Suite 3
Eugene, OR 97401

www.wipfandstock.com

PAPERBACK ISBN: 978-1-6667-4262-6
HARDCOVER ISBN: 978-1-6667-4263-3
EBOOK ISBN: 978-1-6667-4264-0

APRIL 22, 2022 10:28 AM

The closest touch to my soul

Written between 2014 – 2021

Special thanks to all the lights in my life,
you mean the world to me.

you've fallen for my eyes, but they don't know you yet

and dream of me
when you drift asleep
in those deepest parts of the unconscious mind
when your brain shuts off and everything winds
down
i can slip in or have i always been?
closing your eyes on the soul train
switch in to the right lane
everything is right now
i can hold you right now
set your guard to drop
hold your soul
you have mine
see the real me
see the real you
unfiltered now we're whole
you're in my soul
you're in my soul
closing your eyes is the soul train
switch into the right lane
everything is right now
i can hold you right now
we all feel afraid of not being perfect, that's why people connect
don't let that slip away
don't let yourself slip away
that spark can't go out
keep your soul truly lifted
in your arms my face i'll bury
then the world isn't so scary
it's not so scary
and in my heart i know you will stay
you won't slip away
and i know at the end of it

gold

i've got me
don't abandon your own soul
run to my arms it's fine
breathe my soul
i'm just trying to keep that heart of mine
lifted to the sky
i stand up again
i've let you in under my wings
soul on soul
the perfect team
you can see what's under
because you won't harm
these are my safety
i hold myself tight
and i won't drift,
only to sleep
breathe in
the music of the seas
drops in my water mind
breathe out
wrapped tightly
our hearts glow like fireflies
my head is full of songs and beautiful words

chocolate hair falls over tan
shoulders
speckled gold in forest eyes
crescent light that sparks the dark
you can't see what my mind holds
people deaf to soul speak
deep and precarious
like a travel agency my minds a trip
tropical destination
if you wanna get let in you gotta be patient
train station
unpredictability is the inevitability
of my mind
it's a pocket where the soul rests
listless
drifts in and sparks the creativity
in me
heart mind and soul
connected
lifeboat
people deaf to soul speak
but you can hear me
you see through the lies my eyes leak
the colors like melted rain
you can hear me

waves lap the beach at sunset
face down in the white sand
glows red now like a sun tan
and it grows darker as the sun fades
starclan
and finally my mind spills
and finally my mind spills

people deaf to soul speak
but you hear so well
and since you're here, well,
might as well let you in
and you see the story that these eyes leak
the colors like melted rain
waves lap the beach at sunset
face down in the white sand
glows red now like a sun tan
and it grows darker as the sun fades
starclan
and finally my mind spills
and finally my mind spills

paint splashes and Japanese gardens
spilled thoughts and ginkgo leaves
all let go when we stop trying to please

she's unsatisfied,
even though she's gold she's crying inside
waiting for those tears to dry
but if this is the last goodbye,
her heart might just die

had you again
thought it was different this time
had you again
thought our hearts were the same
it's not even the first time
not the first time

here so fast and you're gone again
but that feelings long from gone
thought for a moment had you for a moment
then you up and leave
almost is never enough and it's not even the first time

gold

i guess you guess we guess,
we never really know,
holding back is just a reflex
we're lost in the dark with pretenses

i guess you guess who knows,
we're just cowards that's all it shows

i guess you guess we guess,
we're just the dark before the sunrise glows

i guess
you guess
if words just came to our lips
if we could just open up

then our worlds would collide and we could turn on the lights

we could be the sun starting to rise

aenea kanaan

sprawled out
and songs to melt me down
on the bed like lights out
and you got me down, knocked out
got my heart, lost and found
hold me tight, right we on lockdown
right we on lockdown
and you got me down, knocked out
woke up dreamin now it's dark out

gold

lost time
lost in my mind
lost, frank ocean

stuck in between
hope and despair
half of me in showers,
the other too numb to care

not sure where i went wrong
or the direction i'm going
i just see my chance blowing

was that the finale
is this the end
was this a mistake, or just fate
i can't comprehend

lost time
lost chances too
frank ocean, i may have lost you

sunflowers' heads dropped like they're in prayer
fixed on the ground
like the suns not there
the suns not there

evenings falling now
quicker and colder now
i'm lost and empty now
empty how

i wonder if this is true,
this knowing you

a mind full of unsaid things
a bolder tongue
and we're the castle's stoic watchmen
shaped views from where we've been
we've risen
we're risen

coming out battered and slightly bruised
from a constant cycle
into your hands

blind bravery and cowardice
in the same step
love and hurt
in the same sentence

mango
crescent slice like the moon
soot and dust sit heavy
on my bones
rust breathes on my soul

spring wind combs the trees clean
weight slides off the shoulders
of my mind
i hear whispers of my voice
lost between the drops of gentle rain

oh my soul, don't go alone

gold

sunlit essence
brilliant eyes
oh you take me
to lilac skies

aenea kanaan

fingers run on
delicate curves
warm skin radiates heat
like the sun

moving in tandem
love spilled into the air
dripping, curling
like locks of hair

eyes lock
electric heart, electric pulse
caught in the same breath

creeping silent across the snow
paws soft, claws muted
gentle, sleek steps
clouds stained gray whisper snow
falling lightly like petals blow
a dusty russet coat
covers slender shoulders,
a lone wolf in the night hours
accompanied only by the stars and the still
numb to the cold
with a brain like a midnight pool

what if when i get there,
what if all my idols, my guardians
turn out to be fakes, phonies, frauds
shallow identities trapped in the game
run by everything unseen,
maintaining the illusion that we're in control of our own fates
lies spread and wrapped around our minds,
the world through silicone wrapping
fed to us from your local grocery store,
in your cereal, your saturday morning cartoons, your evening
    news
bred and raised in captivity
no free range in the city
where is the jungle, what is my culture
our wild sedated
only educated to be manipulated
our whole worlds, fabricated

i used to dance in the rain,
blood pumped fiercely in my veins
back when i knew what was real
when we all knew how to feel

wake me at the sunset
don't let me fall back asleep

breathing in the rain,
pulling in slow and deep
take away the pain
wet streets slick
with running streams
auburn buildings from dying rays
lost in thought
and fog wrapped trees
a full stage in front of me
it's radiant in motion
viewed through a screen,
like old anime movies
more than just a video game
these thoughts of mine to blame
can't break my gaze
can't look away
from it passing by

breathing in the rain,
pulling slow and deep
numb these thoughts in my brain
take away the pain

lights on the water
gliding through smooth
a wake of black glass

tenderly lifting paper into air
a light on my fingertips
a breath of starlight and a locked stare

curving gently into pin pricked navy
without a sound
into the great beyond

handfuls of the soul
aloft on the sky's tides
released into heavens arms
free floating ecstasy

see me eyes unclouded
come on and see me

turning the music up to drown out my thoughts
leave no trace
erase my
tabs on tabs
i need to close the windows in my mind
distracted from the present
ripples in muddy pools
and i'm out of the picture
clear is your point of view
oh why can't i just see you?
closing off emotions
but feeling everything
so deep
too deep
i need to meditate

i'm trying i just can't relate
to you
i'm not the same

roll off of me like rain
rollin that body like a wave
in dark music and lights
night life to forget daylight
maybe it won't be the same
maybe it'll change things
in my mind
we drink to erase times
maybe they'll finally be gone at sunrise

wrap me in twilight arms
i don't want to feel anything

heart of gold
a true child from the stars
but her fronts are cold
they all walk away when that shit gets old

patience is a virtue
no one has
she lives in the night life to forget the
daylight
on the search for souls
the same as hers

heart of gold
a true child from the stars

she felt dead and empty. she couldn't help these feelings in her, or
lack of feelings. night brought it out of her. laying in bed alone left
room in her mind, room to think. about anything and everything
there could be. no boundaries in this hour, her mind went far.
reached farther than she wanted into lands she didn't care for and
finding emotions that weren't desirable. thoughts that weren't
friendly.
she was tired, so tired. but she couldn't let herself sleep.

aenea kanaan

balls of light dance on your fingertips
let loose above the sea
fireflies floating in a clear sky
on the night your hand held mine

waves slide across stone
streets interlace across a romanced city
flowers pour out windowpanes
reaching their petals toward starshine

the city is alive in midnight hours
moonlight dances across the streets
and lanterns sing their rays over the sea
wrapped in ocean spray and warm night air

"there's no room for me"
my heart screams, "anywhere at all, i dont have a place even in the
    corners of your mind."
if i could touch your soul it would feel like liquid silver, match to
    mine in gold
dripping over my fingertips
i can't lie, shit fucking gets to me
interlocked energies in front of my eyes,
i'm nowhere in sight
rose gold on a tipping edge
and i want to hold your hands
but i'm slipping away
i don't belong here do i?
scenes flash before my eyes i wish i could speak, words won't
    come to my lips
frozen in numbness
fronting plotting a move
but i'm just sitting here drawing blanks, without you and with
    everything to lose

isolation is my weapon
fronts are my soldiers
walls enclose the palace i'm desperately trying to protect

gold

we met for a reason
we connect for a reason
we left for a reason

if i could, i would pause time to write out my thoughts
all of them
every last drop of rain as it rolls off my pen
post millennials
wrapped in an ocean of blue
i would rather be with you
but this isn't really about love
if i let them all out, would my feelings finally leave?
stretch their wings in the sky
and take flight?
i don't want to sleep anymore
i'm so tired
of dreaming movies

gold

i rose and rose
and i was free

her eyes shut fast, feeling the rush of wetness. threatening to spill over her dark lashes, the guardians of her almond towers, the windows to her deep, amber pools. pools to her real, her truth. that she tries so hard to shield. for anyone who doesn't mean well. only through careful inspection could she hope to tell. her rain builds, in clouds furrowing on her brows, sweeping serenity off her waters and filling the wind with the scent of showers.

"my rain, it's spilling," she breathes. "i can't hold it in anymore."

her eyes fill, pool, and overflow. painting paths down delicate cheeks. running its course around curves. she wipes them, beads dripping down her lashes.

"i always fear it will be too much. that they'll see thunder roll and stay away." her glossy eyes flash up, piercing with an electric gaze. "maybe it's just better that way."

her small body shakes, like a poppy caught in a raging storm. her own storm raged on, contained within a small stem, with petals that caught the wind and furled like sails.

"why close yourself off? would you rather be alone?"

her eyes were glass windows, and he saw her spirit break a bit. "no.. not at all."

he opened his arms,
desperate for her to let go,
for her blossom to open
in the light of day he could be for her

and the world
was at her fingertips.

she appeared carefree, like an open book. but beneath the surface
her fronts stretched a mile wide. around her delicate shoulders,
her hips, and especially her mind.

she fronted on having fronts.

with an attitude that she didn't care, she was confident, self as-
sured. it wasn't a lie, but greatly misunderstood. she did care, a
whole lot. she projected the sides she wanted people to see, but
left out their polarities, the other halves. the self doubt that went
hand-in-hand with confidence. the secrecy that walked beside
her honesty. she cared too much that other people wouldn't know
how to handle it, how to handle her. with no past experience of it
being done, people furthered her existing doubts.

she was wary, and studied her company.

i've grown weary of temporary
in and out of my life
changing like seasons
i want a constant
something i can touch with my
gold fingertips
and believe in

gold

the stars sit in the hills
nestled, gleaming in the distance
like hollywood
they could be anything
you could be
anyone

i want it to burn so intense
like the sun
yet neither of us flinch
or turn away
instead
we stand willing in the flames
because they do not eat us alive
but rather, sustain us
from the inside

why do i care so much to be
beautiful
what is beautiful
is it a color, something i can buy?
does it sit on my shoulders
or cover my eyes?
is it all of me combined
or merely a veil
to gaze through at others
while they, veiled, gaze back at me
not the real me, but the me i chose to present today
the one that's polished, poised
and knows what to say
she's everything anyone ever could want
or desire to be
performing on a grand stage
yet it's not enough
it's never enough
because what's underneath gives a
cry to be heard
the veil is a marvelous, shining net
trapping a bird
which looks out at a world
with soft hazel eyes
and wishes to fly

33

through this short existence
one thing has remained solidified
as an absolute
because of life's constant change
you yourself are the only thing that remains the same

gold

the delicate tiptoe of rain
around the corners of a conversation
and i held my breath
to hear it fall
and your touch
feels like little flowers blooming
across my back

little fish breathe
kissing the surface of the water
the ceiling of their world

my being is like a flower
who bends in the rain
glossy drops sliding down my stem
my fragile petals furled by the wind
and your eyes watch me
wet in the rain
from your windowpane

it feels like i can't be close to people
like every time i try
i'm falling i'm tripping into boundless space
i pull away into myself
i won't look you in the face
i don't like to be weak
i don't like vulnerability
i don't like that you see me
all opened up
i feel incredibly weak
but i know i'm strong
i know that i can stand up and keep carrying on

i feel helpless and lost and
out of control
i don't like how i make myself feel
so small

i want someone to see
the vulnerability
in my body
and keep it in mind when they
touch me
i want them to see my strength
and never pity me in moments of weakness
i want them to deeply
respect my soul
above all
to treat my body gently,
but know i won't be broken if dropped,
just bruised
to know that i could withstand anything they had to throw
i want them to embrace my fire
and step willingly into the passion of my mind
unflinching,
with flames equal to match

aenea kanaan

what does it mean to be free?

i wonder what it would be like
to just be energy
and what job i had or how much sleep i got wouldn't really matter
and i could wander around
as a feeling
feeling things
and connecting with the energy of others
in a world
where time wasn't of the essence
and i was fluid
like a dream

this phone has become a part of me
an extension of my mind, and my hand
i try to rationalize
that i don't need it
that it's the same as it was before
that i only use it for my thoughts
and connection with others
there's a factor of codependency i'm leaving out
an addiction i don't want to talk about
but isn't there with everything?
before notes,
i would have used paper
and before that,
my mind was the sole guardian to my thoughts
my mind feels so big, and changing like the ocean
i'm afraid i won't be able to keep it all in
and remember
it's safety,
security in these notes
that i all but fall apart without
i spill my universe
it's dripping on my fingers

last night i remember
i said music was the only thing that helped anymore
the only thing that could take the force of my emotions
my head above water as light rain drummed the surface
the wind smelled like a storm
but i wasn't scared anymore
i could finally breathe
a lovely pocket of silence filled the air
i was captured in a moment, me and the storm
eye to eye
just my heart beat and the sky's
peace of mind

it happened so fast
all at once
the sky it shook
as the petals fell
sliding from their stem
not gracefully
but in a clump
like that sudden downpour
when the thunder claps
and the skies open

gold

does it matter if i have something to show for it?
or does this journey of experience count as enough
do wisdom and stories
carry the same weight
as awards, numbers or feature films?

in the end how does it feel to be a number?
did you get what you came for
did it satisfy you
finally?
the perfect life
did it give you what you needed?

tell me
why do you feel empty, hollow inside?
lost and alone
at least you have your pride
at least the people know your name
so why aren't you satisfied?

there's no point in being my own enemy
so stop being so hard on yourself
you've always been so critical
learn to be accepting
remember love
written into your back
right at your spine
you need to have yours
save yourself first
no one can do it for you better

love yourself

i want to shut you out like a light
you're too much
keeping me up at night
unnecessary
running your mouth all the time
i wish you would keep quiet
and enjoy the silence
that comes when you
sit still
when your mind
stops
racing

my skin was warm to the touch
almost all the time
except when the last rays slipped under the horizon
and wind off the sea
cooled my bones

i'm trying to figure it out
in the wintertime
it's coming back
bleach and tom foolery
i can feel it, see it
driving through the jungle
but there's snow in my mind
driving on ice
it hasn't been, won't be the same
i'm going through changes
where do we go from here
i don't have you anymore
just memories
you're not here
just your feeling
stuck in my mind like perfume
i blow you to the back most days
but your scent lingers
and gets on everything
some people are like rain
they drip through my mind, changing the scenery
they dry,
but you're worse
your fog clouds my mind
the image gets sharp in music
it's all i can see
existence revolves around negative space
with and without
i'm coping with your absence
an empty space, my without
i've replaced these spots with me, myself
my solace is solo now

i want a give and take
a balance
where we reciprocate
i want to grow together, build something grandiose and beautiful
that satisfies us both
i want to unapologetically be myself and not feel ashamed
as if i've overstepped
i want to be important to you
i'm tired of giving more
always starting over
i'm ready to be close like that
and let our fronts slide
as we stand face to face
soul to soul
without flinching, or moving to hide
truly unfiltered
i want vulnerability to be celebrated
to learn how to be fearless
i want to believe that i'm good enough
whether that comes from myself
or with help
i don't want to feel the nagging grip of insecurity around my
    mind
i want to be cooled, washed away by zen
and peace of mind
so i can sit with myself and know
i'm enough
the first step in self love is acceptance
i want to reach beyond seeking external validation
and be lead by self appreciation

i want to remember what i deserve
so i don't take your shit anymore

i'm not trying to take away your freedom
there's nothing wrong with sharing yourself with someone else
and coexisting
a mutual bond built on trust and communication and honesty
honestly i don't see what the problem is
why i can't have that
why is it only on your terms
why am i in the wrong for wanting more
for asking more, not expecting
i didn't know you weren't willing to let anyone else in your world
i wasn't aware it revolves around you
if you're trying to keep your freedom
i'm not stopping you
i don't see why i can't have a place
but i can't change your priorities
and i'm consistently feeling like i'm not important in that way
when i was ready to give

for some reason i thought that would
mean something to you

i let myself spill
onto this white comforter
sativa with a view of the coast
i leave the room in my mind
and into the sky
where i can dip my toes into a
pool of stars
as i sit on the edge of the universe
like some majestic demigod
i'm really just one soul
on my own
everything else seems so trivial
as i gaze into nothing and everything that ever was
i'm a grain of sand on the shores of the world
i let my worries drain out of my mind
evaporating and clearing my headspace
i breathe you in
everything and nothing
the sun sets on midnight,
the light is never gone
soon, pricks of light dot the ocean of sky
and a new world gleams from the depths of night

it doesn't really matter
but there's so much weight to it
i'm mindless i go dumb
trying to integrate with it
and act like it's a connection
when all i feel is separation
this disconnect inside
fronting on the outside
i keep going back
trying to be satisfied
but you're not it

i want what really matters
to do something that really matters
to me not to you
who the fuck are you
to tell me what to choose

i'm addicted that's really what it is

why are you so desperate to find somebody?
what do you think you'll find in someone else
you know no one else can make you whole
you insist you're whole, so why are you incessant?

i think you're lost
you love yourself but somedays you forget your worth
and your eyes are clouded to the reality of your existence
it shines through when others chime in
and for a moment you see
you had nothing to worry about to begin with
but in low moments you compare and you're blinded to who you
   are

and what you have to offer
and it makes people sad,
it makes you sad
you're lost
lost in your thoughts and it feels like you can't get out
lost on the journey home

gold

i miss you so much it hurts
it aches deep
and it hurts most to think
that you don't even care,
that you're doing just fine

i'm over it
the late nights,
living in someone else's hands
i'm missing my freedom
everything feels the same
day after day
i feel like it's hurting more for me to stay
everything is getting to me
i need to get away

i'm lost in movies and music
anything that distracts my trapped mind
tethered by walls and snow and rules,
a god damn degree
i see everyone else living their fantasy
in comparison i'm breaking myself down
in reality most are no better than me
and glamorous lives are all but real
i live to create my reality

i'm not my best self
as of late
i'm not who i want to create
my head is lost in daydreams
of beautiful people and beautiful beaches
splashed in miyazaki-like sketches
you're not like me
you don't like me
cuz i'm not easy to figure out
not like everybody else

i find myself inside staring at the sky
at sunsets of lavender and touches of rose

gold

i'm drowning my sorrow in rosé
this medicine doesn't fix anything in the real world
none of this actually matters
in the real world

you didn't close your eyes
but you closed your mind
you've closed the door and
shut me out
i'm locked outside
as your castle walls tower high
left in the dark,
blind to the light of your thoughts

the way it happened was like a light switch,
so fast you didn't even realize
you're scared to let someone in,
but now
you've made enemies with the wrong side
what are you really afraid of?

i see through a window,
a light left on
with your wary face
peering outside
and i saw through the gaze
of those emerald eyes,
everything you've tried to hide

i thought that was what i wanted
it's like drinking to forget someone
keeps it at bay
but we all know that doesn't do the trick
wake up feeling like pushing everyone away
i don't want anybody's company
but my own
and those that know me truly
craving, needing
that connection

i don't want these people
can i please melt into your arms
just for a bit

i'm finally here
i planned this cocktail party
and you're the last to arrive

i love you in your nikes
with your hair messy
and your favorite hoodie

your essence is most important
someone will love you for you

gold

this feeling is eating away at my stomach
unease creeping through my insides
unconsciously present
i don't want you here
i didn't invite you
but the feeling has arrived
my head is spinning
my heart quickens
trying to locate the source of this
anxiety
it feels like someone dropped marbles
in my head
and let butterflies loose
in my stomach

reaching to distract
trying to bring my breath back
sinking into the sheets
trying to regulate my heartbeat
i feel it beating in my rib cage
wings pounding for my attention

i care about you so much
it hurts
and i'm kicking myself
because it's so hard for me to tell you
i've let the sun come down
without letting you know
just how much you mean to me

i love the soft part
right under your eyes
a silk canvas
when tears slide
into silent pools
lovely lily pads under your eyes
softer and gentler
than anyone's words
have ever been towards you

this bourbon tastes just like you
basements and sly shit
laughing so hard it hurts
it's right there
i'm right back there
winter nights on flights of stairs

my heart beat is racing
just snuck in safely
i'm high on you

from the first night
backs against the bridge
a head full of stars
a new chapter begins

didn't know if i would ever see you again
it's wild how the universe works
i dodged two bullets
and landed at your feet
looking into those amber eyes
haven't met your kind
i'm faded, high
on you
it's just begun
are you feeling it too
faded
it feels so goddamn nice
with you holding my thighs

didn't once think
you'd noticed me
didn't once think
that we could be

faded on you
faded i'm gone

gold

it would be so funny
if this was something we laughed about
down the road
let it all go
is it funny now
all the time we spent stressing
or i did
will we ever

on the beach
you and me
sunbaked
we're losing it

what if through all this
we held on
what if all this
was a little lie

would you realize?

you'll hear stay
you just want
what you can't have
no way

falling for you
the clouds are falling
for you
take my hand

look up look up
the sky is falling

i miss who i thought you were

i miss fantasizing,
dreaming, imagining about secret societies
living in the trees
or the stories that i would hear
on the midnight breeze
before 77 million things ran on my mind
all at the same time
before when my mind had space to
breathe
and soared free on the skies
i miss when what we call "an escape"
was my reality
when the only thing on my brain
were endless possibilities for clan names
before every day became the same
trapped in this endless monotony of trying to find time
but it always slipped through the cracks
of my outstretched fingertips
i miss my mind feeling limitless
like it could stretch for miles
and never burst at the seams
when a play date never seemed long enough
and now we're waiting for the time to be up
so we can rush to our next appointment
no longer a pleasure
but a chore
"that's life"
but does it have to be?
what about my childish mind that begged to differ
and show me how life could be
with all the beautiful possibilities
before we all had our grown up problems with our grown up jobs
and we all forget about the time before we grew up

rain on the air
swept off my feet and into the wind
but you're not here

so tell me something i don't know
gazing into those flames
when will you put it all down
and stop with these games

mango on my lips
and the wind in my hair
i'm ready to go anywhere

as long as you're here

sunsets in my drop top
pull up in my sweats
slim lil body in a crop top

if only you could ride for me
ride for me like you'd die for me
if only you could ride for me
that's how it should be

ride for me
it's more than that
we could be

treat me like a lover
love me like no other
even though you might not be here after

waiting on the winds of change
surprise me in your light
and tell me your heart's right
smoke in the air
can't tell me how you feel
hood up, tuned out
don't you know how to be real
let me be on your mind

what a funny thing to be
i won't lose sleep
over someone who doesn't even dream of me

gold

bonfire under the stars
you took my hand
you've got my heart

grab my face
and pull me close
don't let go

when i go
it won't be for long
it's still hard
but i won't go far

pinky promise you
i'll always come back
pinky promise you
to break your back

amber and green
i melt in your gaze
for you, i'm quite keen
i just can't stay away

i'd like to find my way back
if you're ready, that is

hold out on me and go on a limb
for the chance we'll be together again

i don't want to worry you'll grow weary of me
or that the depth of your care,
was really quite shallow
to begin with
in the end, it was my hopes that were quite steep

but if for a second
you could hold on tight
and into the arms of faith we leap,
falling quite fast
right through the clouds
your hand in mine,
down we soar
but never afraid
when i am where you are

gold

why has it become so hard to love,
and so easy to hide?

had to recover myself tonight
off the front lines
pull me back
into my own arms

who's hurt you?
i'll be there for you
always here for you

and i wish i could trust you with my secrets
if i could let down my guard
unload my arms
could you hold it?

can anyone take care of my heart
like i can?

gold

i'll give you the same energy
i have to make myself a priority
if others won't

never gonna hear my heart break
even when you don't reciprocate
spending my energy on you
never know if i'll get it back

it's a gamble i'll make
trying to use me for my light
that's not yours to take

what does it take?
how much of me do i have to give
to join that circle of yours?
how much will i have at stake,
before you put your heart in the game
what do i stand to gain
from being the only one in the game
it's not fair
it's not fair to be the only one
giving and giving all this time
you might not see it,
everything i do
how much i care

don't play with my emotions
i meant it when i said
i was invested
oh how down i was
for you

how much will you take?

this is what words can do
this is what the world can be
expand what you believe is possible
and the universe rises to meet you

i'm quite honestly sick of this cycle
i've grown weary of this dance we do
but never of you
that's why it's so frustrating
constantly caught in the in between

we know what's between us
why can't we be us

i can't have what i want
and neither can you

i'm weary of you
i'm weary without you
i'm tired of pushing you away
for now you can stay in that studio apartment in my mind
keep taking up rent space
in this heart of mine

stepping back from you
to take time to tend this garden of mine
weed out the shadows
and water the light
helping it grow
it doesn't happen overnight
but in time i can take you there
walk these paths i've designed
to my favorite spot
in the heart of the plot
going within showed me the power i hold
to transform a tiny seed
into a beautiful garden
tiny but mighty
they're not to be taken lightly
and now it's finally ready
i hold your hand tightly,
to show you something you'll like a whole lot
with petals like golden hour
they've grown up like towers
and turned their faces to the sky
my sunflowers

kindness matters. integrity matters. the truth matters.
not everyone has the same heart as you, don't forget that

and there's nothing wrong with having a heart that actually works

gold

seeing you for what i want,
but who are you really?
can i ever see anyone clearly
dreamed up a version of you
and i love them dearly

hold you so close
i see you behind my eyes
under pastel skies
bathed in pink hues

matte black wings rest on shoulder blades
dusky skies and locked eyes
shielding my light
you make my heart glow

worlds shattered
when our worlds collide
and the you i thought i knew died
right in my arms
right in my mind
but i can't seem to let you go

your taste lingers on my lips
one i never knew
and i can't let it go

aenea kanaan

and she fell in love, for real this time

open my heart like a butterfly
you don't know just what it takes
it's not what i'm used to
but i saved a seat for you,
anyway
a moon landing in these emerald eyes
and for the first time
i can't look away
i just hope you won't pass me by

i don't have words for this
i haven't been here before
everything about you is magnetic
i fell for your soul

gold

tears glistening on my lash line
like fresh snow
seeing the world from the sky
i'm in so deep it's insane

spent every second with you
and i still can't get you out of my brain
i don't think i could ever grow weary of you

i don't want to miss a second
i don't want to forget how you felt
i got you, and you got me

posted up in emotions
you got my little heart thumpin
hoping maybe this could be
something
hoping this could be
everything i need
holding my breath

i've had all this love
and no one to give it to
waiting for the right place
the right time
to find mine

open my eyes and you're right there
opened my heart and i'm all yours

i lost my head, lost my mind
on the coast of malibu
it's peace of mind
but i long for you
your touch, your embrace
just give me a taste

you got me impatiently, waiting
just tell me, i'm waiting
i'm faded, i'm hit
like a drug i'm off it
these games you're not playing
i'm sick that i like it
i just hope that you're staying

our love language fit perfect
we go rounds, it's a circuit
just tell me, you're worth it
you start it i'll finish
with you i stay winning
i'm sick that we're twinning

i'm elated, glad that i waited
look at this world we created
for you i'm so faded
got me so wasted
i just wanna taste you
everyday i'd still take you
love how soft i make you
but even softer for you
i could melt in your arms
on a cold night you're still keeping me warm

me and my baby we just vibe
catch us on the interstate
we just drive
we like to live large
feeling alive

money on your mind
freedom on mine
see how much time money can buy
don't even gotta worry with you,
the way time flies
on a new kind of high

my heart and soul
me and mine
my love you're divine
always my sunshine

i wonder if you can feel me thinking about you
all the time

i smell like versace
these hoes try and get at me
tell em don't at me
you don't even know me
thinking you can pull me
talk to my homie, my man
he knows me
we're not even associated
sick that you're waiting
as if this is changing
on the sidelines
a bench warmer
but you stay hating

piece of me inside those eyes
i love how you slip away without saying anything
i'm feeling dramatic
all i'm hearing is static on the other end
a mouse has cut the wire
and i'm stuck in my head

lost in those honey melon skies
that i keep dreaming up
amber behind my eyelids
did i dream you up too?

call you so softly
i wish that you heard me
but deep down i'm worried
you don't feel it,
not how i mean it
no reason to worry
you tell me, reassure me
but this feeling won't leave me alone

gold

told you be honest
you told me i fuck with you heavy
you don't know what that meant b
i'd keep your heart if you let me

it's the light that i chose
i'd go through hell and back for you

i still want all of your love
give it all to me
my heart is yours to keep

spent a lot of time alone
and i know it's helped me grow
feels like that's all i know
when i really wanna go home

and i know i should be grateful
there's so much that i take for
granted
things that fill me up
but lately i'm feeling like the only one
that's really here
in the nighttime
and it's hard to see you
when i'm calling in the night
can't you come through?

gold

i want you so bad
i'm really just fiending
when i'm sleeping
and it's not really you that i'm seeing
at night when i'm dreaming
everything is not what it's seeming

my feelings for you run deep
river run deep run wide
run the night with you by my side

can i tell you how i really feel?
so down bad and it's all for you

the depth of my feelings for you is unimaginable
in the skies of my daydreams
you're all i'm thinking about
and in the starshine behind my eyes when i'm asleep
you're running and running through my mind
don't you ever get tired?
i hope you never stop coming around

it's an honor
to have you spending your time on me
have a seat, please stay awhile

gold

i feel the tides within me
rolling and crashing like waves
i have no more tears left to save

off it
and i'd still hit
but you don't love me the way i do

lost it
and i want you
talk to me like that's all i got

all i got
shining on me
all the things you're not
in the moonlight
i see you so clearly

do you want me
say me
i'm the one you choose
but i know it's not real
you're all for appeal

save it
for someone who believes you

finally feeling secure in my own presence

sometimes i get scared to share you
like letting the world see how amazing you are will somehow take
    away
from the place i hold in your heart
when i breathe in love
i realize what a silly fear that is

one of my favorite things about you
is that you're not for everyone
i don't mean your personality isn't suited,
you're one of the most charismatic and charming people i know
no, i mean you guard
who you let close to you
similar to how i do,
not just anybody has a seat at the table
picky about company
you're not for the streets
and so i know you're sweet on me
just for me
you don't know how special that leaves me feeling
all for me cuz i'm all for you

one of my favorite people you know

i'm in love with the peace we cultivate
and our passionate debates
you take all of the cake
and show me the love
i'd just dreamed of touching
only moments before you
it feels like worlds away now

gold

why do i still be getting scared
watching my surroundings
keeping covered
it's taking me there
no matter if i'm loved up
it still keeps coming up

give me your hand
and take mine
take me somewhere my mind won't go
take care of me
help me breathe
let me let go

i hope you can take me there
get me high
lift me up on air
and i see you acting like you care
put it on
that's all on me

i think you might be the one for me
and i hope you don't take that lightly
give me the goosebumps
my skin tingling on this flight
miles away but your heart is right here
mine stays with you
nothing changing that
everything i meant,
stays the same, no take-backs

still arguing that violence is self defeating
king said it best
far from the solution
but that's why i watch what i'm eating
what you put out comes back to you
that's why power is fleeting
it comes from greed,
a fear of lack causes you to take more than you need
living in fear will leave you stuck there
and tear you apart inside as you compromise
bending over backwards to keep up with the lies
that got you on top
selling your soul for a quick fix
to get rich

is it worth it
you don't see price tags
you don't see what it cost you
don't notice you lost you
until it's too late
for nobody does time wait
and now it's a losing battle
from rags to riches
feeling impressive but something's still missing
when you're alone, in the night the thoughts follow you home
because you forgot who you were
left it behind
in the race to secure your spot
and now you can't find peace

all at once
triggered from past harms
tears slid instantly
as i crumpled into your arms
you were horrified
of the damage you thought you caused
it's never happened with you
i watched you react
as i fell back in that place
before i knew your touch
my mind raced
i was numb and so exposed
but i didn't push you away
i wanted you to stay
as i sobbed into your arms
whispered in my ear i was safe
always safe with you
your tears were warm on my cheek
heard you calling my name
urgently
because you never meant to hurt me
my heartbeat was slowing
it matched yours perfectly
my feet met the ground and i sank into you
the trust i put in you was all i was knowing
my faith in you never fell through
even after everything i been through
you find a way to get through
touch my deepest reveries
i'm just like a book you love to read
i never have to front with you
you see me
and i see you

gold

always come back to me
over and over again

lately it's a lot to process
i need a release
between you and me
it's overwhelming
these notes are my process
giving my thoughts room to breathe
it's an outlet
gotta let these feelings out somehow
they can't pay rent no more

gold

which is more important,
    getting or letting go?

love you so much it hurts to think about
if one day i lose you
when we're old and stuff
i'll still have a crush
i'll stay if you'll have me
until we have to say
goodnight
for real
in my bag real down bad
to think about all the times we've had
i don't think i could ever grow tired of you
in the slightest
that's why i'll hold you the tightest
while you're mine for some time
but deep down i wish you would stay
so down bad and it's all for you
genuinely don't know what i'd do
without you

gold

unfocused
not yet hopeless
under quiet skies
i saw it in your eyes
the light just about died
nobody was home
but just then
a cinder caught kindling
it flickered and restarted in amber
a warm glow returned
as your fire burned

love me forever
tell me we'll always be together
until it's the last time i breathe
just tell me i'll see
you again

gold

It was beautiful, and I loved every second of it.